KID-POWER!

The Holy Spirit's Super Power for Kids!

KID–POWER!
The Holy Spirit's Super Power for Kids!

E M Publications
P.O. Box 780900
Wichita, KS 67278
www.enloeministries.org

International Standard Book Number: 978-0-9794331-0-8

Printed in the United States of America.

Second Printing

1

Who in the world is the Holy Spirit?

Who is your favorite super hero? Have you ever wished that you could have some special super-power to help people?

Well guess what? You can! There is someone who wants to give you this power, and His name is the Holy Spirit!

So who in the world is the Holy Spirit? That's exactly the question some people asked Paul in the Bible: "We haven't even heard that there is a Holy Spirit" (Acts 19:2).

Before you can have the Holy Spirit's power, you need to know a few things about Him.

Did you know that the Holy Spirit is God's Spirit? The Bible tells us that God is different from us in seven special ways.

1. First of all, He never had a birthday!

God has always been around and He will never go away.

2. God knows everything! That means He knows every secret and can never be tricked by anyone.

3. God is everywhere! Even though you can't see Him, He is always everywhere. That's how big He is!

4. God has all power! That means He is stronger than Superman and can do anything.

5. God is perfect and never does anything bad! The Bible uses the word

By Barret Enloe, age 4.

"Holy" to describe Him. Holy means perfect.

6. God is also very loving! In fact, the Bible says that He is love. God loves us all so much!

7. The last way that God is different from us is that He shows Himself to us in three different ways—as Father, Son and Holy Spirit.

God the Father is the one who sits on the throne in heaven (see Matthew 6:9).

God the Son is Jesus who died on the cross for us and came alive again (see Romans 1:4).

God the Holy Spirit is the one that helps us here on earth now (see John 16:13-15).

If you love God, the Holy Spirit has already been helping you in many ways. Let's look at some of them now.

2

How does the Holy Spirit help us?

There are five ways the Holy Spirit helps us:

1. The Holy Spirit helps us to know right from

wrong (see John 16:8).

When we're in our rooms at night and turn out the lights, it can suddenly become dark and scary. When we do bad things, our lives get very dark. The bad things we do are called sins and they turn out the lights in our lives. The Holy Spirit helps us find the switch to turn the lights back on so that our lives are not dark anymore. Now we can see the right things to do.

The Holy Spirit turns the light on when we ask Jesus to forgive our sins. Each time the Holy Spirit helps us see what we've done wrong, He also helps us make things right!

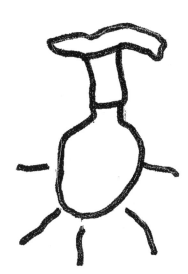

By Barret Enloe, age 4.

2. The Holy Spirit makes us new inside (see Titus 3:4-6).

Have you ever played in the mud? You probably had mud all over your hands, feet and clothes–maybe even in your hair! How did you get rid of the mud? You took a bath!

Sin makes us dirty inside, but the Holy Spirit is the one who washes us clean (see Titus 3:5). The Bible says that everyone has "sin-mud" inside (see Romans 3:23).

When we ask Jesus to forgive our sins, that's when the Holy Spirit washes us inside. Then we are clean from all of our "sin-mud".

KID-POWER

By Braedon Enloe, age 10.

13

Have you ever asked Jesus to forgive your sins? Are you all dirty inside? If you ask Jesus to forgive your sins right now, the Holy Spirit will wash away all of your "sin-mud" and make you clean inside. Why don't you ask Him now and pray this prayer?

Father God, thank you for loving me. Please forgive me for my sin-mud. Thank you for sending your only Son, Jesus, to die on the cross for me. I believe that Jesus came alive again and still lives today. I want Jesus to live in my heart. I love you, God! In the name of Jesus, Amen.

3. The Holy Spirit lives in us (see Romans 8:9).

The Holy Spirit also helps us by living in us. Remember when you took your bath and got cleaned up from your "sin-mud?" That's when the Holy Spirit started to live inside your heart. Everyone who asks Jesus to forgive his or her sins has the Holy Spirit living inside.

Since the Holy Spirit now lives inside of you, that means He's always with you. The next time you're scared or confused, remember that the Holy Spirit is not only with you, but lives in you!

By Dolan Enloe, age 7.

You know how when a new school year begins things are a little scary? You have a new teacher, a new classroom—even new kids to meet. You don't walk into that school alone, you bring the Holy Spirit with you!

You are never, ever alone because the Holy Spirit is always with you.

4. The Holy Spirit helps us to be more like Jesus (see Galatians 5:22-23).

Have you ever noticed when you hang around kids that are doing bad things, that it is much easier to do bad things with them? On the other hand, when you hang around good kids, it is easier to do the right things.

Now that the Holy Spirit lives inside of you, He hangs out with you all the time, and that makes it much easier for you to do the right things.

The Bible tells us that the more we let the Holy Spirit help us, the more we can become like Jesus. The Bible calls this "the fruit of the Spirit."

> *But the Holy Spirit produces this kind of fruit in our lives: love, joy, peace, patience, kindness, goodness, faithfulness, gentleness, and self-control* (Galatians 5:22-23).

It's called the fruit of the Spirit because

By Barret Enloe, age 4.

19

it grows like fruit on a tree—and it will grow in your life too!

5. The Holy Spirit will give you power.

The Holy Spirit will give you power to do great things that you can't normally do. Have you ever wanted to tell one of your friends about Jesus so they can go to heaven with you? The Holy Spirit can give you the power to say the right things to them. The Holy Spirit can also give you the power to pray for your friends when they are sick.

You may have thought that the Holy Spirit and His power were just for grown-ups,

By Braedon Enloe, age 10.

but the Bible tells us that even kids can receive His power:

> *"In the last days," God says, "I will pour out my Spirit on all people.   Your sons and daughters will prophesy"*
> (Acts 2:17).

Hey, that's you—sons and daughters. It's not just grown-up power; it's KID-POWER!

The word prophesy simply means to say the words that God wants you to say.

Are you ready to hear more about the Holy Spirit's power now?

22

3

What is the baptism in the Holy Spirit?

We just talked about what the Holy Spirit's power can do in your life. He can give you courage to tell other people about Jesus and give you power to pray for them too. Jesus said the Baptism in the Holy Spirit is how you get this courage and power:

> *But you will receive power when the*
> *Holy Spirit comes upon you. And you*
> *will be my witnesses, telling people*
> *about me everywhere—in Jerusalem,*
> *throughout Judea, in Samaria, and to*
> *the ends of the earth* (Acts 1:8).

You know how when someone is baptized in water, they get all wet? When you're baptized in the Holy Spirit you don't get wet, you get POWER—power to help you do things you thought were impossible. With the Holy Spirit's power, you can do anything God wants you to do.

By Dolan Enloe, age 7.

There are two great things that God gives you when you are baptized in the Holy Spirit. You get to know Jesus better and you get that power we just talked about.

One of the names that Jesus is called in the Bible is the "Baptizer" in the Holy Spirit. You already know Jesus as your Savior because He washed away your sins with the Holy Spirit's water, but now you can know Jesus in a new way.

When you are baptized in water, you get drenched in the water. When you're baptized in the Holy Spirit, Jesus drenches you in the Holy Spirit.

Have you ever done a "cannon ball" into the deep end of a swimming pool? How wet did you get? Just a little, or were you drenched? Chances are you were soaked—there was water all over you! When you're baptized in the Holy Spirit, you get soaked in the Holy Spirit and His power is all over you.

From then on, the Holy Spirit's power to help others is always with you in a greater way than before!

By Dolan Enloe, age 7.

4

Who can receive?

The only thing you need to be baptized in the Holy Spirit is to know Jesus as your Savior.

In the Bible, everyone who received the

Spirit's power already loved Jesus. That means that if you've asked Jesus to forgive your sins, you are ready to be baptized in the Holy Spirit right now!

No matter what you've done or what's happened in your life, as long as you've asked Jesus to forgive your sins, He's ready to baptize you in the Holy Spirit now.

Do you like to get presents on your birthday? Did you do anything special to earn those presents? No, you were simply born on that day. Jesus wants to give you the gift of the Holy Spirit simply because you've been born again—not because you did anything special.

By Barret Enloe, age 4.

5

How do you know when you have received the Holy Spirit's power?

What's the last thing you bought at a store? Was it a toy? Was it a video game? When you paid for it, what did the cashier

By Braedon Enloe, age 10.

hand to you? A receipt, right? The receipt is proof that this new item belongs to you now. It's all yours! God wants to give you proof that the Holy Spirit's power belongs to you.

In the Bible, when people received the Holy Spirit's power, God gave them proof. Let's look at some scriptures together:

> *And everyone present was filled with the Holy Spirit and began to speak in other languages as the Holy Spirit gave them this ability* (Acts 2:4).

> *Even as Peter was saying these things, the Holy Spirit fell upon all who were listening to the message. The Jewish*

believers who came with Peter were amazed that the gift of the Holy Spirit had been poured out on the Gentiles, too. For they heard them speaking in tongues [other languages] and praising God (Acts 10:44- 46).

Then when Paul laid his hands on them, the Holy Spirit came on them, and they spoke in other tongues and prophesied (Acts 19:6-7).

What was the proof that God gave people in the Bible? That's right, it was that God helped them to speak in a brand new language they had never learned before. The Bible shows us that when you receive the Holy Spirit's power, you will also speak in a brand new language.

Why in the world would God want you to speak in a new language? Remember the Holy Spirit wants to give you the power to say the right things to your friends about Jesus. The baptism is all about God giving you the power to say the right things!

If you can trust God to help you speak words you don't understand, you can also trust Him to help you speak to your friends about Jesus. This new language is your receipt, or proof, that you now really have the Holy Spirit's power.

6

How do you receive?

First of all, God really wants to give you the Holy Spirit's power! The Bible helps us to see how easy it is to receive this gift.

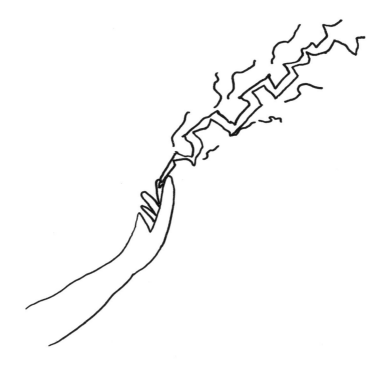

By Dolan Enloe, age 7.

There are three simple steps to receive the Holy Spirit's power:

1. First, you need to start talking to Jesus out loud. Remember that Jesus is the one who soaks you in the Holy Spirit.

So, what should you say to Jesus? Open your mouth and tell Jesus how much you love Him. Thank Him for dying on the cross for your sins. Ask Him to give you the Holy Spirit's power.

If you want the Holy Spirit's power, you need to talk out loud to Jesus first.

2. Second, something incredible happens when you begin to talk to Jesus. You'll begin to feel the Holy Spirit's power on you. This is the way Jesus shows us that He's ready to baptize us in the Holy Spirit's power.

This is just what happened in the Bible:

Then when Paul laid his hands on them, the Holy Spirit came on them, and they spoke in other tongues and prophesied (Acts 19:6-7).

Sometimes it takes a few minutes of talking to Jesus before the Holy Spirit's power comes. But other times, He comes right away. Whenever He comes, you'll know it!

3. Third, when you feel the Holy Spirit's power come on you, it's time to speak in your new language. But how do you say these new words? The answer is in the Bible:

> *And everyone present was filled with the Holy Spirit and began to speak in other languages as the Holy Spirit gave them this ability* (Acts 2:4).

When the Holy Spirit's power came on people in the Bible, they opened their mouths and began to speak out loud. But when they spoke this time, the Holy Spirit gave them words to say that they didn't understand. He will do the same thing for you.

The first step we talked about is something you choose to do. You choose to talk out loud to Jesus.

The second step is something Jesus does for you. He sends the Holy Spirit's power on you.

The third step is something you and the Holy Spirit do together. You begin to speak the new words that He gives you.

Remember when you first learned to ride your bike? You sat on your bike and

By Braedon Enloe, age 10.

44

grabbed the handlebars, but your feet were still on the ground. Then somebody kept you from falling while you began to pedal. Your helper didn't pedal the bike for you, they simply helped you to not fall down.

When the Holy Spirit comes on you, He's there to be your helper. Just like learning to ride your bike, you and your helper each have a different job to do. Now, you have to do the talking, but the Holy Spirit will give you new words you've never learned before.

7

It's time to receive!

Are you ready? Let's do it! It's time to receive the Holy Spirit's power!

Let's start by asking Jesus to forgive us

46

for anything bad we've done. That way we're sure our hearts don't have any "sin-mud."

Don't forget the three steps to receiving the Holy Spirit's power: first, start talking out loud to Jesus. Second, the Holy Spirit's power will come on you. Third, you speak out loud the new words the Holy Spirit gives you. Okay, here we go!

1. Let's start talking to Jesus out loud now. Why don't you ask Jesus to give you the Holy Spirit's power. Tell Him how much you love Him. Thank Him for dying on the cross for you. Don't stop!

Jesus loves to hear you talk to Him out loud!

2. Jesus will send the Holy Spirit's power on you. It might happen fast, it might take a few minutes—that's okay. Keep talking to Jesus out loud until you feel the Holy Spirit's power.

3. Now it's time for you to say the new words the Holy Spirit is giving to you.

Remember how we talked about learning to ride your bike?

By Dolan Enloe, age 7.

You had never ridden one by yourself before, but somebody helped you. Now the Holy Spirit will help you say the new words you've never said before.

Now is your time to start pedaling by talking, and the Holy Spirit is going to help you by giving you the brand new words.

Once you begin to speak the Holy Spirit's new words, thank Jesus that He gave them to you. From now on you can pray with these new words whenever you want.

If it's not happening for you right now, that's okay. Sometimes it takes a little while. There's nothing wrong with that. You can pray and ask Jesus anytime you want. It will happen soon if you keep talking to Jesus about it.

If it has happened for you, that's awesome! You've received the Holy Spirit's power! But there are a couple of things you still need to know.

8

How does the Holy Spirit's power help you?

You know how you were just speaking new words that you didn't understand? Are you wondering what your new words meant?

When you speak these new words, the Bible says you are praising God (see Acts 2:11) and praying to Him (see Romans 8:26-27). This is an awesome way to talk to God, and you can do it anytime you want.

Have you ever thought it was hard to tell your friends about Jesus? Now that you have these special new words from the Holy Spirit, you can be sure that He will help you know what to say to your friends about Jesus. Isn't that cool?

The more you pray to God with your new words, the braver you'll become to tell your friends about Jesus in English!

KID-POWER

By Barret Enloe, age 4.

9

What now?

Hasn't this been fun? You got to know Jesus in a brand new way. He drenched you in the Holy Spirit, and you began to speak in a new language just like the people in the

By Braedon Enloe, Age 10.

Bible.

From now on the Holy Spirit's power is always with you. You can talk to God in your new language whenever you want. In fact, why don't you try to pray in your new language for a few minutes every day? This is a great way to stay full of the Holy Spirit's power. It also helps you remember that God will give you the right words to say when you talk to your friends about Jesus.

Remember, the Holy Spirit's power is all about giving you the right words to say!

Why don't you try to talk to someone about Jesus today? The Holy Spirit's power will be right there to help you say the right words to them. Go for it, you can do it!